Let's Explore
Needs and Wants

by Laura Hamilton Waxman

BUMBA BOOKS™

LERNER PUBLICATIONS ◆ MINNEAPOLIS

Note to Educators

Throughout this book, you'll find critical-thinking questions. These can be used to engage young readers in thinking critically about the topic and in using the text and photos to do so.

Lerner Publications Company
A division of Lerner Publishing Group, Inc.
241 First Avenue North
Minneapolis, MN 55401 USA

For reading levels and more information, look up this title at www.lernerbooks.com.

Library of Congress Cataloging-in-Publication Data

Names: Waxman, Laura Hamilton, author.
Title: Let's explore needs and wants / Laura Hamilton Waxman.
Description: Minneapolis : Lerner Publications, [2018] | Series: Bumba Books™—A first look at money | Audience: Age: 4–7. | Audience: K to Grade 3. | Includes bibliographical references and index.
Identifiers: LCCN 2018004065 | ISBN 9781541538528 (lb : alk. paper)
Subjects: LCSH: Money—Juvenile literature. | Basic needs—Juvenile literature,
Classification: LCC HG221.5 .W39 2018 | DDC 332.024—dc23

LC record available at https://lccn.loc.gov/2018004065

Manufactured in the United States of America
1-45035-35862-5/23/2018

Table of
Contents

Let's Go Shopping

Look at this money!

You can buy things with it.

What will you buy?

You can buy a toy with money.

You can buy a snack too.

A toy is fun to play with.

It can make you happy.

But it is not a need.

Food keeps you healthy and strong.

Your body must have food to grow.

Food is a need.

Clothes are another need.

They cover you up.

They keep you warm.

What else do you need to live?

A game is a want.

You may like to have it.

But you can live without it.

Candy is another want.

Many kids like candy.

But no one needs candy to live.

What are some of your wants?

Families buy things they need first.

They buy food and clothes.

They spend money on a place to live.

Sometimes money is left over.

Then families can buy something they want.

They have fun together!

Needs or Wants?

Look at the pictures below. Point to what you need to live. Then point to the things that are wants.

Picture Glossary

money

bills and coins
used to buy things

need

something you
must have to live

spend

to use money to
buy things you need
or want

want

something you
would like to have
but do not need

23

Read More

Bullard, Lisa. *Lily Learns about Wants and Needs*. Minneapolis: Millbrook Press, 2014.

Pistoia, Sara. *Money*. Mankato, MN: Child's World, 2013.

Shoulders, Debbie. *M Is for Money: An Economics Alphabet*. Ann Arbor, MI: Sleeping Bear, 2015.

Index

Photo Credits

Image credits: Amy Salveson/Independent Picture Service (money icons throughout); imagestock/E+/Getty Images, pp. 5, 23 (money); Blend Images/Shutterstock.com, p. 6; Tetra Images/Getty Images, p. 9; Jose Luis Pelaez Inc/Blend Images/Getty Images, pp. 10–11, 23 (boy eating sandwich); HelpingHandPhotos/E+/Getty Images, p. 13; djedzura/iStock/iStock/Getty Images, pp. 14–15, 23 (playing checkers); Roman Stetsyk/Shutterstock.com, p. 17; Steve Debenport/E+/Getty Images, pp. 18, 23 (grocery store); Image Source/Getty Images, p. 20; Photodisc/Getty Images, p. 22 (salad); restyler/Shutterstock.com, p. 22 (Chinese checkers); supachai sumrubsuk/Shutterstock.com, p. 22 (ice-cream cone).

Cover: Hal_P/Shutterstock.com (groceries); M. Unal Ozmen/Shutterstock.com (ice cream).